meadowdrama

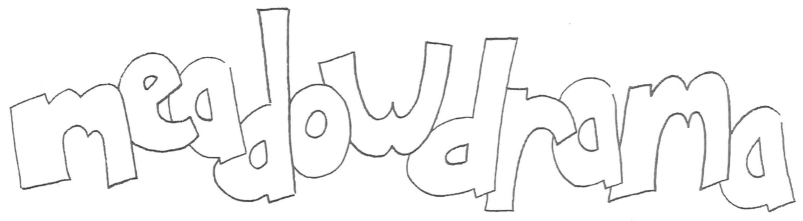

Ben Hertel

Outskirts Press, Inc.
http://www.outskirtspress.com

ISBN: 978-1-9772-3676-0

PRINTED IN THE UNITED STATES OF AMERICA

Meadowdrama is dedicated to my mother, Lynne Hertel,
an amazing woman who loved to laugh, and didn't have
a mean bone in her body.

Serious Fiction

meadowdrama
Ben Hertel
what the HELL is wrong with you?
Pardon me?
well, you're so nice and friendly...
That's bad?
I have learned over time to hate almost everybody.
I like you.
my point exactly!...
only an idiot would say they liked me!
... maybe like is too strong of a word.

meadowdrama

Ben Hertel

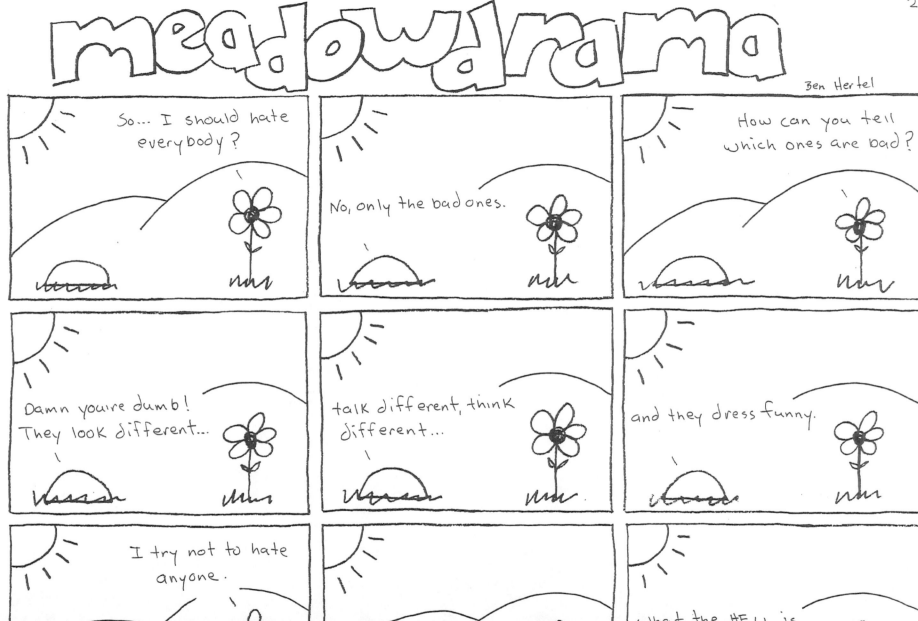

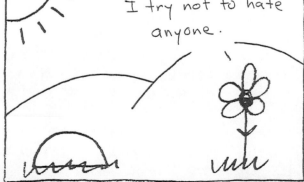

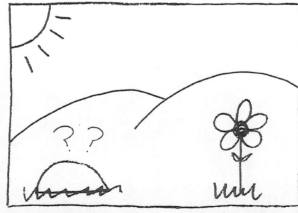

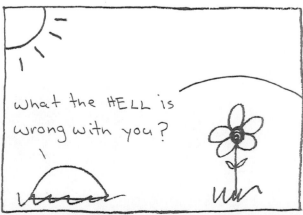

meadowdrama
Ben Hertel
I always try to give grace when I meet someone.
Grace? Who's that?
Not a person... I mean –
I assume someone is good when I meet them.
That's CRAZY talk!
Folks will screw you every chance they get!
maybe you only see in others what you see in yourself.
And what's THAT supposed to mean?!
Dang, reaching this guy could take a lifetime.... or two.

meadowdrama

Ben Hertel

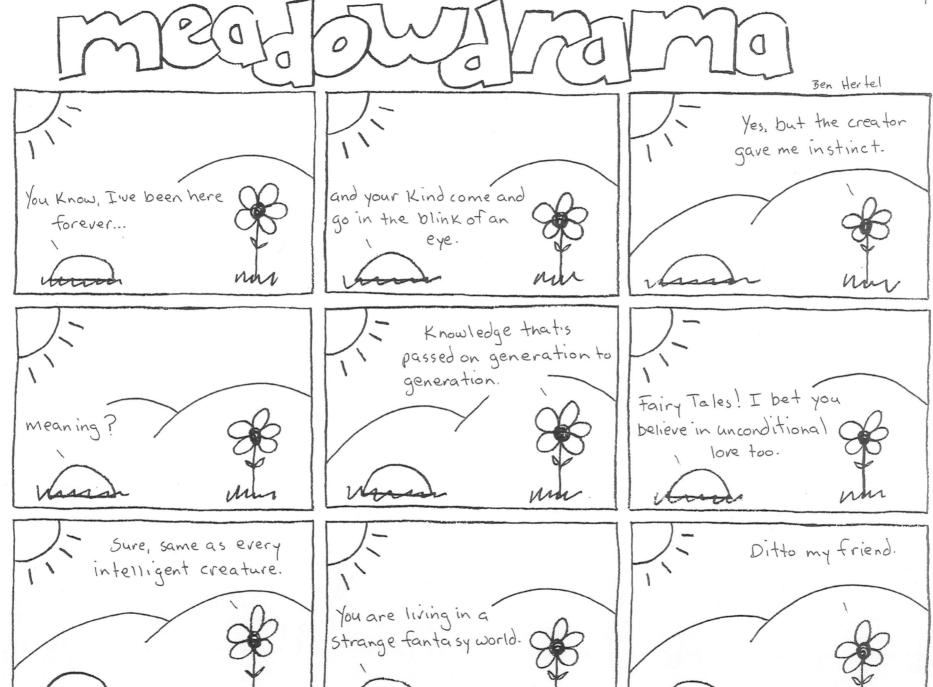

meadowdrama
Ben Hertel
First, I'm not your friend.
Second, you and all your Kind can fall over dead for all I care...
Third, Keep all that hippie-dippie love crap to yourself!!
You are so D-U-M!
um...
you forgot the B.
That's another thing I hate...
BEES!
How could anyone not love bees?

meadowdrama
Ben Hertel
Hey rock!
Will you shut up!
But I-
Shut!
I just-
up!
shut up, shut up,
SHUT UP!!
Weird...
It's like he's trying to tell me something.

meadowdrama
Ben Hertel
Is it better if I speak softly?...
I'll try to keep my voice down so you don't get so upset.
Okay?
What an idjet!
It's the words bumble brain, not the volume!
They make me want to explode!
STOP! SAYING! WORDS!
um....
idjet?

meadowdrama
Ben Hertel
So. idjet is short for idiot or ignoramus.
Oh, I get it.
No. No you don't...
If you did you would never open your mouth again.
Hmmm....
mmmm.....
Hhhhmmmmm...
mmmmmmm...
well crap. That's worse.

meadowdrama
Ben Hertel
Whatever T-Rex, just leave me alone.
Good, I don't like fighting.
T-Rex?
Oh yeah, you wouldn't know...
T-Rex was a ferocious dinosaur, a monster...
with a great big head, and tiny little arms.
YIKES!!
Wait... are you making fun of how I look?

meadowdrama
Ben Hertel
You shouldn't make fun of how someone looks...
it's mean, it's hurtful, and...
this is how the creator made me.
Awww... sounds like T-Rex has some shallow roots to go with....
his GIANT head and teensy weensy leaves.
You are one ornery rock.
Oh... well...
you know...
everybody needs a hobby.

meadowdrama

Ben Hertel

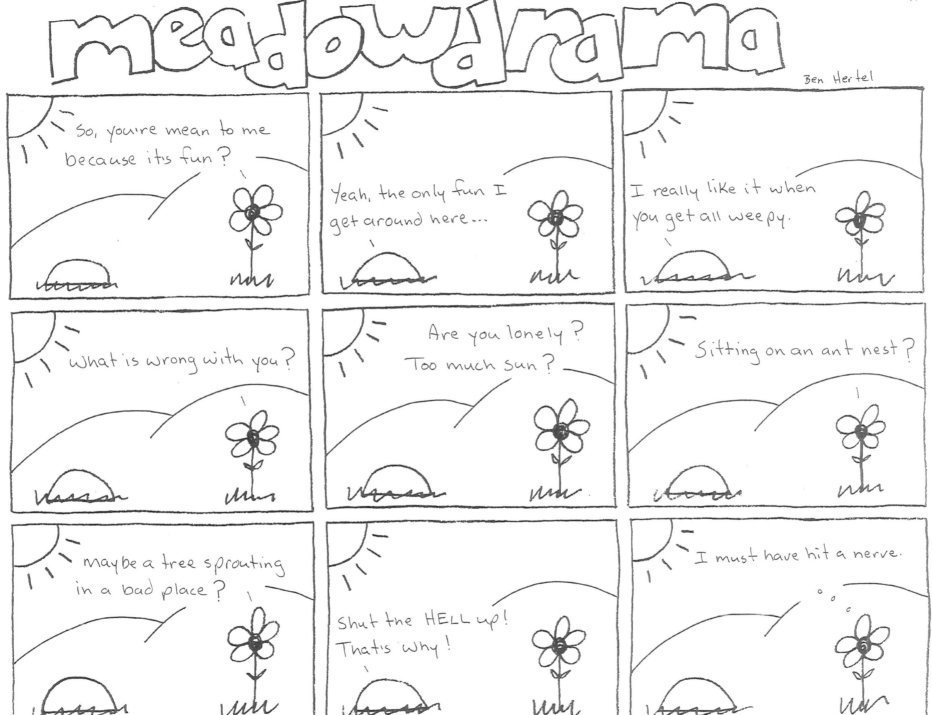

meadowdrama

Ben Hertel

There must be one thing we can agree on.
well... I do like it when the sun warms me up.
I love the Sun!
Except... that's when all you yappie bastards sprout....
with all your 'life is beautiful, and love your neighbor' crap...
I hate the Sun.
No... But... Wait...
Can we start over?

meadowdrama

Ben Hertel

You must have lots of bad Karma...
you Know...
because now you're so angry and unhappy...
and such a potty mouth.
Did you call me a potty mouth?
well... yeah.
HA HA HA HA HA HA HA HA HA
I don't get it.

meadowdrama
Ben Hertel
You can't swear!
I don't like saying bad words.
But it feels so good!
I can help you get started... listen -
Your mom was so ugly she had to pay bees to land on her!
oh yeah!... Well, you're just....
just...
Poopie Stupid!!
oh never mind....

meadowdrama
Ben Hertel
Figure it out fuzz face, life is hard.
Life is glorious!
No. It's harder than hell.
Okay, you think life is hard...
and you're hard....
you know...
because you're a rock....
so.....
What the HELL are you talking about?!

meadowdrama
Ben Hertel
What I'm saying is... you think life is hard...
AND you're hard...
Yeah, I got that part.
Which makes your thoughts..
and physical self similar... so......
Nope...
Still don't get it.
Hhmmm... dense too.

meadowdrama

Ben Hertel

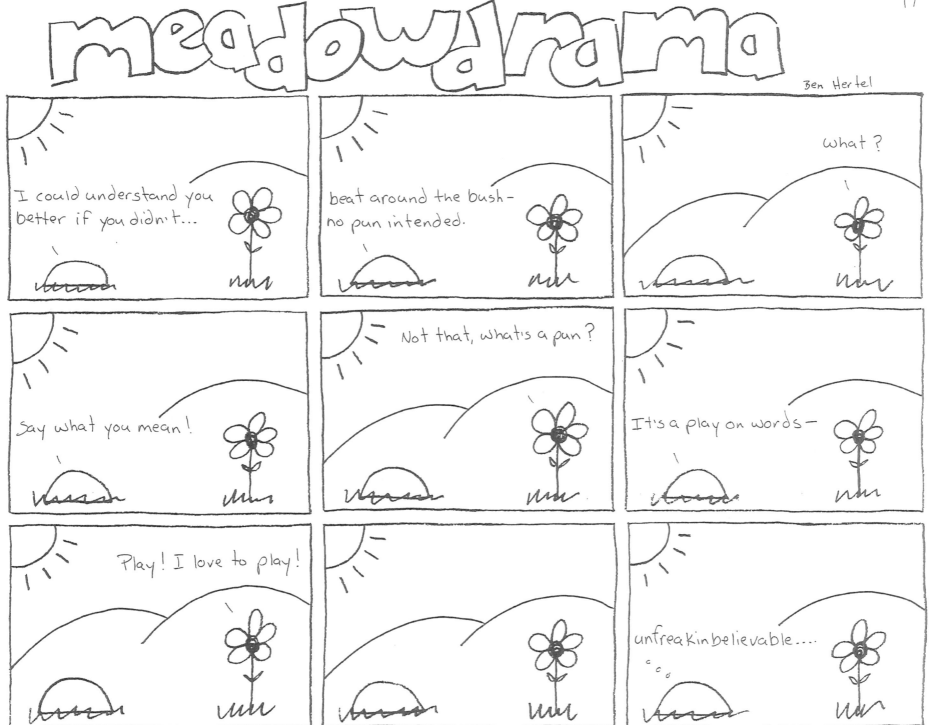

meadowdrama
Ben Hertel
I want to smash you into tiny bits...
THEN grind those bits to smithereens!!
Wow! That would hurt...
and I want to get all the flowers in the meadow..
to dance around you singing songs to help cheer you up!
DAAAUGH!
.... meaning?...
communication is hard.

meadowdrama
Ben Hertel
Still mad?
I'm sorry...
for whatever I said...
I wasn't trying to make you angry.
?
Hello?
Up yours chlorophyll breath!
I'm sure he means that in a good way.

meadowdrama

Ben Hertel

Hey I know! why don't we look at the clouds...
and tell each other what we think they look like.
wouldn't that be fun?
Every time you open your mouth...
I hate you a little bit more.
You didn't mean that - right?
I really, really meant it.
But...
I'm trying so hard!

meadowdrama
Ben Hertel
Hey rock, it's my birthday today! Isn't that exciting!
what? You just sprouted.
I know, I've already been here 4 whole days!
I want every day to be my birthday!
Well, I was born about 4 billion years ago.
wow! we're both 4!
NOT the same thing!
well anyway... tomorrow is my birthday! Isn't that exciting!
and so begins another headache.

meadowdrama
Ben Hertel
You have no concept of time!
You can't compare days to billions of years.
Okay then, what about this moment?
No other time is really real - is it?
Maybe time is only one, long, moment.
What a load of B.S.!
Except...
whenever he starts yammering...
every moment feels like an eternity.

meadowdrama
Ben Hertel
... and I know time seems linear, but really it's more circular...
Kind of an extended here and now—
Shut the hell up!
I've had enough of your psycho-science.
How could you know anything about time?
Instinct, remember.
Sounds more like a long ride on the crazy train to me.
That sounds fun!
Besides... anyone who thinks they're not crazy is crazy.

meadowdrama

Ben Hertel

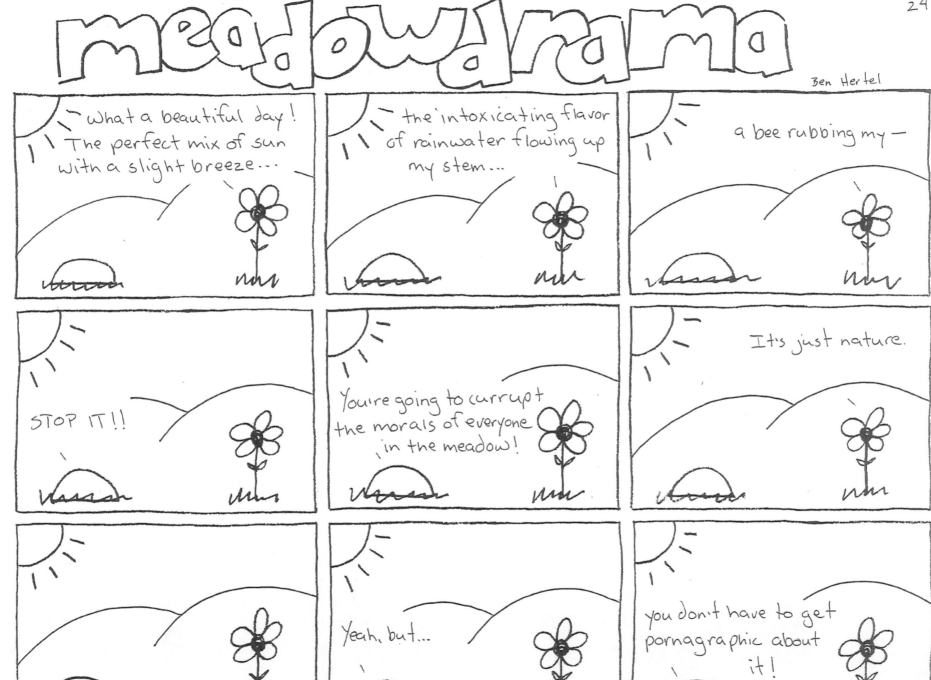

meadowdrama
Ben Hertel
I think you're jealous.
In your dreams stamen face.
I get to breathe the air...
sway in the wind...
grow from the sun...
drink the water...
Whoops...
I think he's crying.

meadowdrama
Ben Hertel
Hey rock, I'm sorry...
I wasn't trying to bum you out...
it's just with your attitude sometimes I'm not as nice as I should be...
all your hostility...
you know?
Cram it pollen head!
Damn flowers...
you're all the same.
Dude.

meadowdrama
Ben Hertel
Did you call me a prude?
No, 'dude' which is very different.
Never heard of it.
It's something you say...
to a friend—
Whoa, whoa, WHOA!
Don't forget, I hate your guts.
Got it.
If I had 'em, you'd hate 'em.

meadowdrama
Ben Hertel
I'm sure you have a soft side...
you were a little sad the other day.
Me? Sad? HA!
I know there's goodness in you.
What a moron!
Are you new around here?
Oh yeah... you are!
I'm sure deep down he has some good qualities...
but he hides them well.

meadowdrama
Ben Hertel
You know, you don't always have to be so macho...
being vulnerable can show strength too.
Vulnerable?
I'm harder than HELL! Indestructible!
But... you must have feelings.
True...
my loathing for all things green.
well... I guess...
That's one feeling.

meadowdrama
Ben Hertel
stupid flowers!
You pop up and start telling me about life...
what's good, what's real, and how great love is....
and I say, Bah Humbug!
You're right, I'm young...
and I think we all need more love in our hearts.
The only love I'm feeling is for the day you fall over dead.
I think someone needs a hug.

meadowdrama
Ben Hertel
A hug? What's that?
Well, we would get close and embrace...
then take a moment to feel the life force in each other.
That sounds AWFUL!
You mean touching?
Yes! I would lay my head on you and give you a squeeze with my leaves.
Great...
now I'll have that image...
stuck in my head for the NEXT 4 billion years.

meadowdrama
Ben Hertel
Well, once again...
I hate you more now than I did a few minutes ago.
Love and hate are two sides of the same coin.
Where on Earth do you come up with this crap!
It's not crap. Love and hate are full of passion.
I just want to squeeze you until your face falls off!
See? You're full of passion.
I think he's starting to like me.

meadowdrama
Ben Hertel
You're starting to like me, I can tell.
?!
Did you get kicked in the head?
Suck up some pesticides?
It's okay. I kinda like you too.
So.....
are you smoking?
Oooo... I hope there's fireworks next!

meadowdrama
Ben Hertel
Dude! I didn't Know you could get so hot!.....
and all that smoke... are you alright?
Listen carefully...
I do NOT like you, you are nuts....
a total blithering idiot!
DIRT has more brains than you do...
NOW! SHUT UP!
Hhmmmmm....
not the Kind of fireworks I had in mind.

meadowdrama
Ben Hertel
I'm glad we're talking again.
WE are not talking, you are talking...
because you can't Keep your fly hole closed...
you, "mr. Fancy Grass," are nothing....
nothing but a deer snack waiting to happen.
Tomorrow you could be a little pile of deer poo.
HA! I love it!
Well, I guess I should be thankful...
no mixed messages from this guy.

meadowdrama
Ben Hertel
I guess if I end up nourishing a deer...
I'm good with that, we all need a purpose.
So far your only purpose seems to be making me so angry that...
I want to jump up and down and tear my hair out!
??
I mean if I had any hair and could jump up and down.....
...I feel bad, but...
I would love to see THAT!

meadowdrama
Ben Hertel
What's your purpose?
Shut up.
No really, what do you think?
Well... after a long life...
I got dumped out here in the meadow...
where all you chatty bastards pop up and spew nonsense...
So, I guess my purpose is to be miserable for the rest of time.
Okay. How can we make that more fun?

meadowdrama
Ben Hertel
Maybe you could learn some stuff while I'm here.
crap... I hate learning stuff...
I'd be happy to teach you.
you!? Like what?
Oh, I don't know, tolerance, humility, respect...
and how important it is to love yourself.
Love myself!?! Are you kidding me?
No, really —
I don't even LIKE myself!

meadowdrama
Ben Hertel
Of all the gobbledygook that falls out of your mouth...
Saying I should love myself takes the cake!
Yeah, it can be tough.
Tough? It's ridiculous! Impossible! So what...
I should stare at my reflection and feel all warm and fuzzy?
No, that's vanity.
Well, you'd have to be one vain S.O.B. to love yourself!
Wait... he can't be right - can he?

meadowdrama

Ben Hertel

Love and vanity are not the same thing...
one is selfish, one is selfless.
Whatever, it's all the same to me....
besides, I'm comfortable being miserable...
and don't want to change.
?!
What?....
He likes being miserable?

meadowdrama
Ben Hertel
so, you're miserable... and want to stay that way?
I'm loving the sound of you not talking...
music to my ears.
!?
How could you like being angry and miserable!?
I didn't say 'like' bumble brain...
I said 'comfortable.'
still... don't... understand.

meadowdrama
Ben Hertel
You're comfortable being miserable?
That's right.
But... you could change, you could be happy!
I don't think so.
um... yes, you could.
No, I couldn't.
YES! Yes you could!
NO! No I couldn't!
This won't end well.

meadowdrama
Ben Hertel
You suneaters will never understand...
I may not be happy, but I don't need any thing or any body...
which is fine by me. So, enjoy your bugs,
wind, and rain. I don't need them...
and I don't need YOU!
Ouch.
You'd better toughen up kid.
Hey, I'm tough...
tougher than any flower out here!

meadowdrama
Ben Hertel
I think I'm starting to understand you.
Stop right there!
AND, don't try to play analyst either.
But, I -
I don't want to know why I think the way I think...
But, I -
OR, why I'm the way I am!
Okay...
So... how's that working for you?

meadowdrama

Ben Hertel

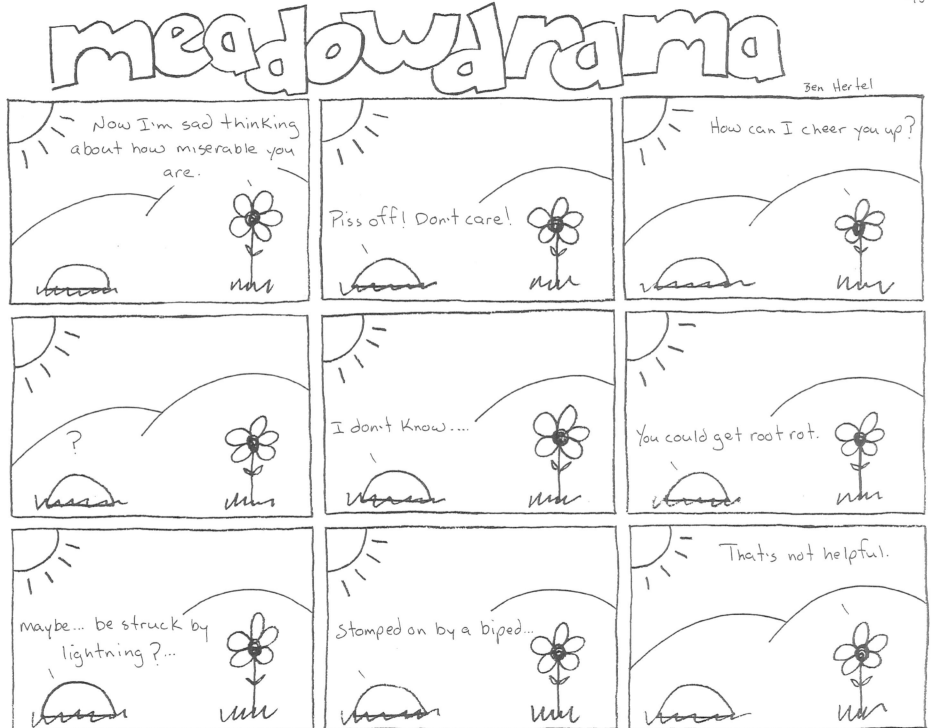

meadowdrama

Ben Hertel

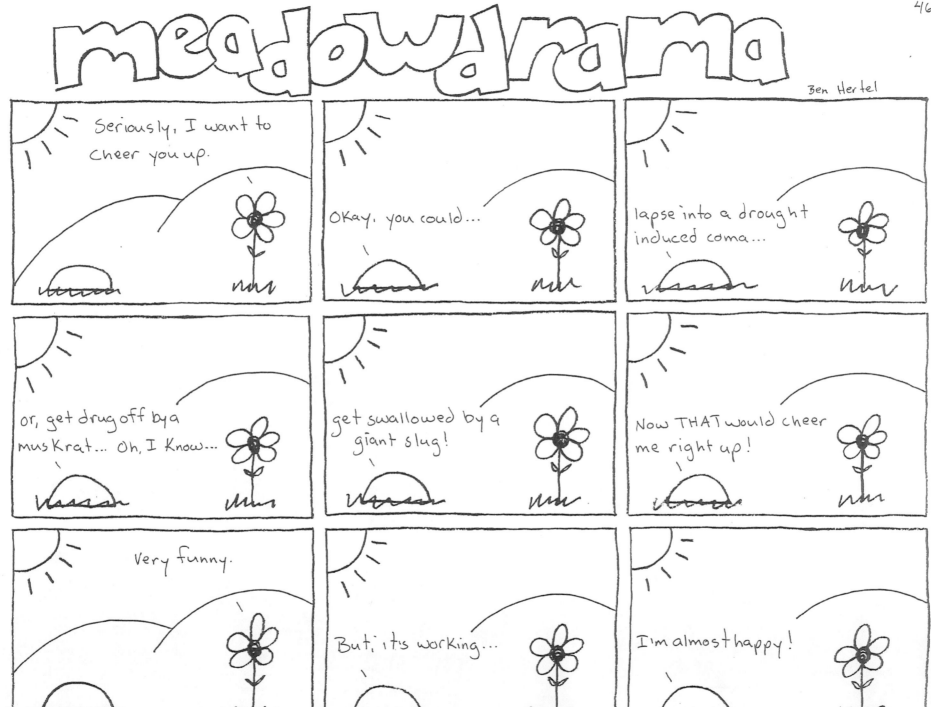

meadowdrama
Ben Hertel
This is more fun than riding that glacier.
You went for a ride?
Yeah, I was born a long way from here...
the glacier picked me up, and dumped me here.
Wow! You are blowing my mind!
Glacier? Never heard of it, how can that be?
The old instinct stops when things get cold don't they?
Cold?....
That dosen't sound good.

meadowdrama

Ben Hertel

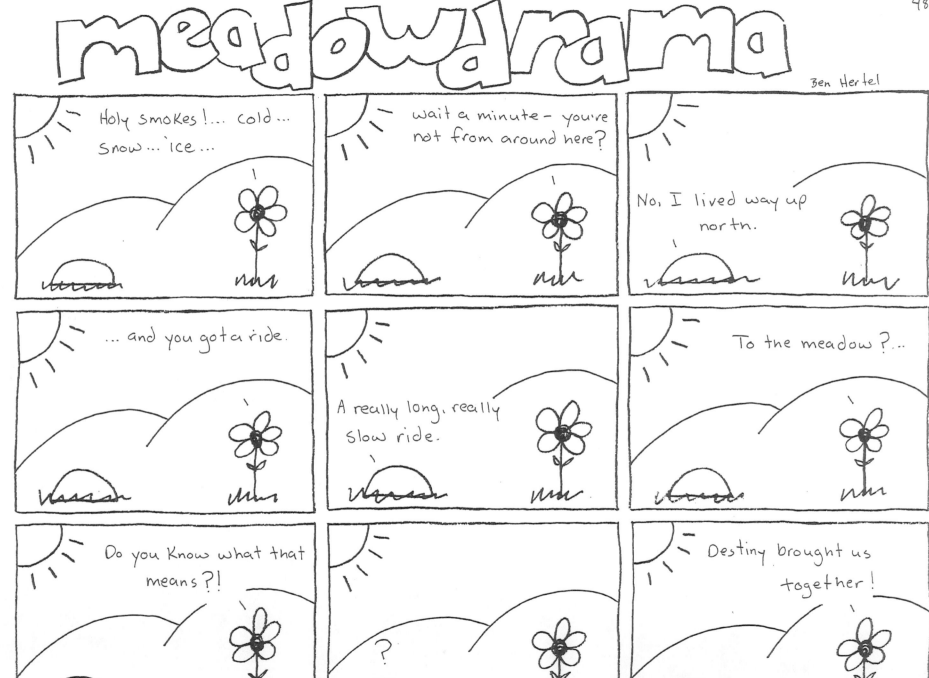

meadowdrama
Ben Hertel
Fate did not bring us together!
I was here long before your kind showed up...
AND you're only here because some stupid bird...
Flew over and dropped some seeds.
I think everything happens for a reason.
Great! More voodoo logic.
You have to face the facts...
you and I are here on purpose.
Facts! What facts!?

meadowdrama

Ben Hertel

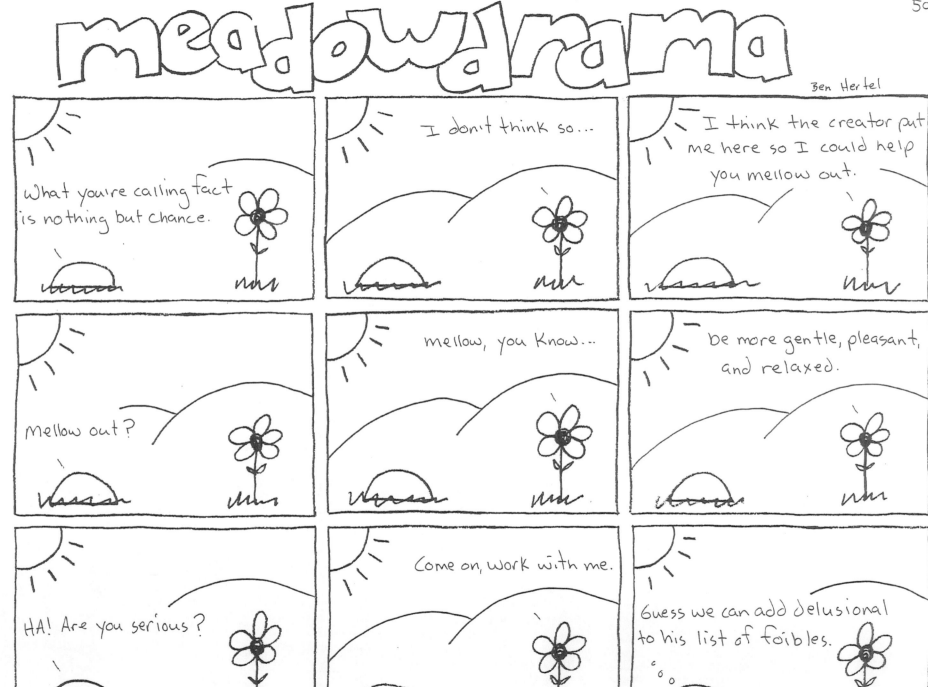

meadowdrama
Ben Hertel
Hey rock, do you want to hear some thing?
Don't care, don't want to Know, not listening.
It's pretty exciting!
Do me a favor for once, and just shut up!
Okay.
?
Now can I tell you?
!!!
Well, when I woke up this morning there was a robin pulling on a worm and I said Good morning. and he said Good morning... Then he was telling me about these people down on the other side of the meadow
and they were all sitting around on a Blanket talking
then the ro heard one of them say

meadowdrama
Ben Hertel
... and if you say 'what a beautiful day' one more time...
I'll scream!
But... look at all that blue sky...
listen to the birds singing!
Boring. Noisy.
I can hear the bees out in the meadow...
sigh....
what a beautiful day!
I heard that!

meadowdrama
Ben Hertel
I've been thinking. you're a lunatic, so it dosen't matter what you say...
it's all gibberish, and I'm not going to let...
anything you say bother me anymore.
Very interesting...
So, how does that make you feel?
DAAAAUGH!!
Now that was a cry for help if I ever heard one.

meadowdrama
Ben Hertel
Listen, we all need help sometimes...
come on bro, let a little love into your heart.
Bro?
First dude, now bro?
Un huh.
How about this - take your 'bro'...
and stick it where the sun don't shine!
? ?
um... Alaska?

meadowdrama
Ben Hertel
I think something is bothering you...
you've been really wound up lately...
super cranky.
I'm not CRANKY!
Well, you sound cranky.
you should stop thinking so much - what you should do is...
unthink everything in that bug infested brain of yours!
unthink?

meadowdrama
Ben Hertel
maybe I have been a little wound up lately...
talking about the glacier reminded me...
everyone else in my family fell off along the way...
and I got dumped here by myself.
What a bummer.
Yeah...
I guess that makes me exotic.
Erratic too.

meadowdrama
Ben Hertel
Sorry to hear about your family. were you close?
We were part of a mountain...
but over time fell apart.
I guess that can happen to families.
Not like that dirt breath...
I'm talking about earthquakes, volcanic eruptions... like that.
Wow! That's harsh!
!!?!
THAT'S WHAT I'VE BEEN TRYING TO TELL YOU!

meadowdrama

Ben Hertel

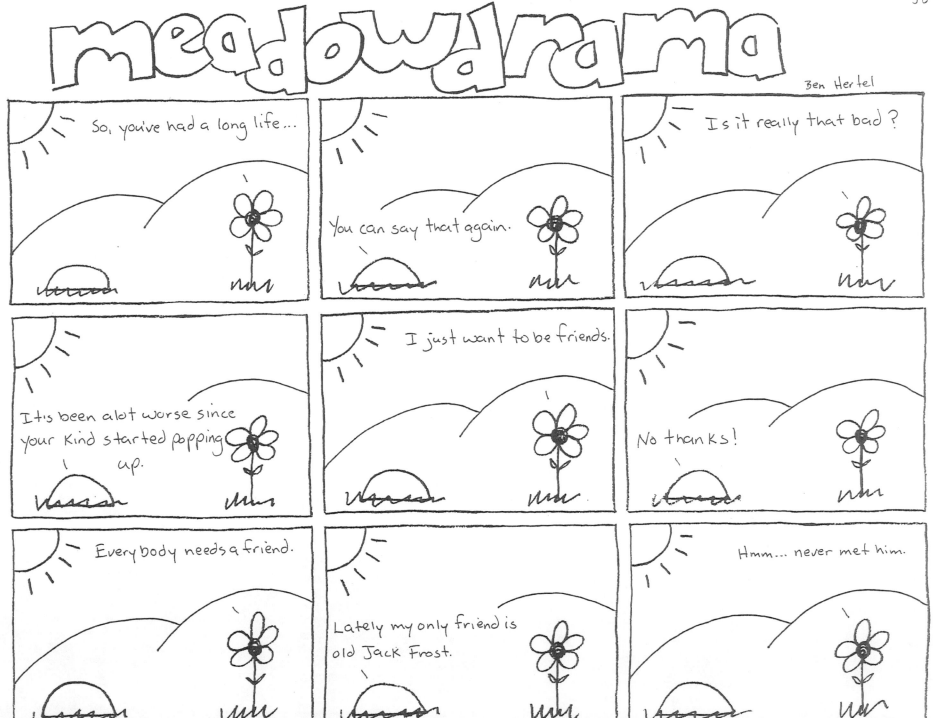

meadowdrama
Ben Hertel
Yeah old Jack Frost creeps in one night...
and freezes you so bad you wake up dead.
Dang... that would be sad.
For you. For me it's...
the start of many happy days...
no bugs, no birds, and no flowers!
Until spring.
I can't hear you!

meadowdrama
Ben Hertel
Good morning!
Do NOT start with me today!
I am so done with your B.S.!
Swooning over bees, the sun, the rain...
telling me how beautiful everything is!
I don't care! You're ugly! I hate you! Shut up!
Dang...
Sometimes he's so mean...
I can feel my roots wither.

meadowdrama
Ben Hertel
Why don't you like me?
What's to like?
Well, we're all made from the same life force.
That makes all of us brothers and sisters...
with people, animals, plants...
even flowers.
No way! That's awful!
Bro.
Not! Your! Bro!

meadowdrama
Ben Hertel
Rock... you can't fight Mother Nature.
Yes I can, I've done it my whole life.
And ?
Shut up and leave me alone!
Dude, just relax, let go...
and rest your weary head on our mother's bosom.
!!!
Crap...
there's another hideous image I'll never get rid of.

meadowdrama
Ben Hertel
Hey, let's play a word game! I'll say a word, and you say the first thing you think of.
Ready? Here we go... Sunshine!
You
Birdsongs!
Are
Rainbows!
Stupid
Hmm... guess I didn't explain it very well.

meadowdrama
Ben Hertel
I Know, let's see who can not talk for the longest.
That game is no fun.
well, I hate fun.
Dang... you're sucha "Gloomy Gus."
I'd rather be that than hyper-happy like you...
you're lucky I'm here...
you should thank me.
what? why?
Somebody has to balance out all your happiness.

meadowdrama
Ben Hertel
You can't really —
Yes I can!
Come on, you —
take your waterlogged brain, all your...
sun crazed happiness, then...
dig a hole... jump in...
and cover yourself up!
I think we're having relationship issues.

meadowdrama
Ben Hertel
We're having relationship issues ?!
I think so... yes.
WE are not a couple!
Sure we are, we live right next to each other.
maybe we should talk about it.
Maybe You should take a deep breath and hold it until you turn blue.
??
I've always wanted to be blue...
who knew it was so easy?

meadowdrama
Ben Hertel
You're the one with a problem.
me?
Yes! You're too happy!
Wow. How can anyone be too happy?
I don't know... with all the crap we have to deal with...
maybe....
I think we're meant to be happy.
Not true!
I'm living proof!

meadowdrama
Ben Hertel
Don't you love the smell of a spring morning?
So new, so fresh...
Not new...
How come?
It's the same damn day over and over...
I'm beginning to think there's only one day...
and we keep reliving it forever.
Oh my! Like being in a nightmare.
Welcome to my world.

meadowdrama
Ben Hertel
Rock, rock, rock, you are so funny...
sometimes I start to believe you don't like me...
then I remember we're all part of Earth's family-
So that can't be true!
Oh, it's true fuzz face.
Right - and I extremely dislike your rocky hard heart...
rocky head, and stoney face!
Are you trying to make fun of me?
making fun is hard...
when you don't have a mean cell in your stem.

meadowdrama
Ben Hertel
Oh my. what a lovely sun filled sky.
?
The songs of the birds, and calming croaks of frogs...
all alive in the vibrant beautifulness of the meadow!
Um... did you crack?
No, I just wanted you to hear what you sound like...
especially after your lame attempt to make fun of me.
I don't sound like that...
but I did enjoy the 'vibrant beautifulness' part.

meadowdrama
Ben Hertel
It's funny that what you hear is so different from what I say.
Nothing is wrong with my hearing.
maybe... but then...
you are misremembering what I say.
I don't think so...
dude, the words may be mixed up, but the meaning is the same.
?
You called me dude, you like me!
Crap... that was a mistake.

meadowdrama
Ben Hertel
Cool, you called me dude.
A simple mistake...
un huh...
I didn't mean it.
Un huh...
Don't worry, I still hate you.
Un huh...
a little Freudian slip?
No! Not Fred's ship! Whatever that means.

meadowdrama
Ben Hertel
I said 'Freudian slip'...
it's when you say what youre really thinking by mistake.
Whatever.
I may have misspoke...
but my hearing is great!
I hear exactly what I want to hear.
I see...
that explains alot.

meadowdrama
Ben Hertel
Interesting... you only hear what you want to hear?
It helps keep me sane.
How so?
It protects me because some of the things you say are so absurd....
my brain wants to jump out of my skull...
and run away screaming!
Dang, we may be more alike than I realized...
because...
I SO feel the same way.

meadowdrama
Ben Hertel
Hey rock, can you hear that?
No, what?
It's the sound of another beautiful day!....
I don't hear anything.
and I can smell the love from all creatures living on Earth...
a symphony...
sigh...
I think someone has had too much to drink today!

meadowdrama

Ben Hertel

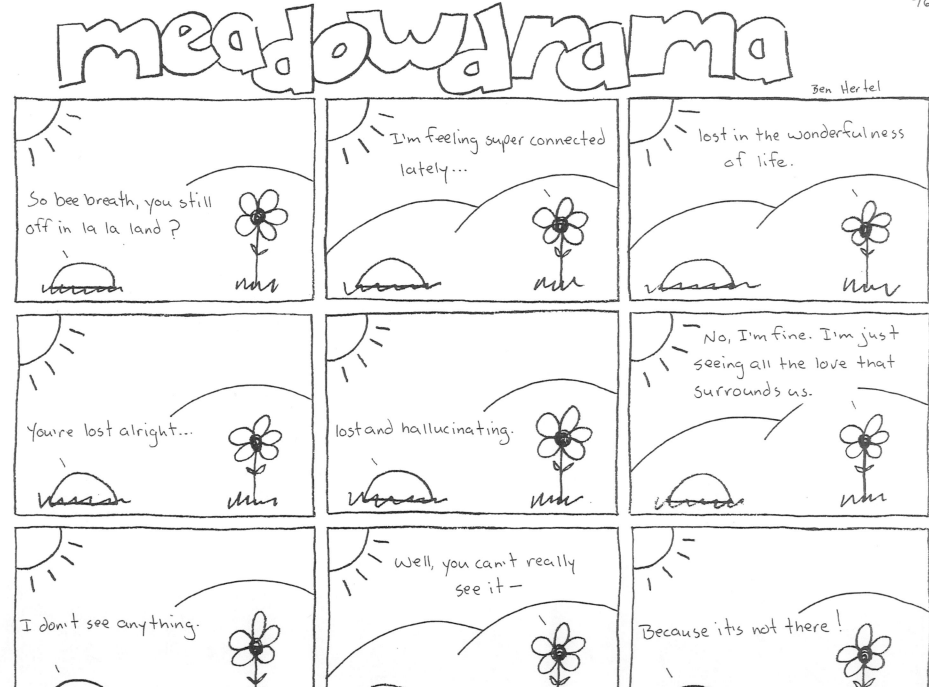

meadowdrama
Ben Hertel
You can see and smell love ? Really ?!
Well...
not literally - but why not ?
why not !
Because out here in the real world, all I see...
is, strife, misery, and hard ship.
I agree...
? ?
that's all you see.

meadowdrama
Ben Hertel
Well, you've lost me again.
Dude, if all you look for is the bad stuff...
that's all you'll see.
That's what's out there!
True, but...
everything is out there, you need to look with an open heart.
Okay... I'm looking...
but all I see is...
a stupid flower child.

meadowdrama
Ben Hertel
Flower child?
That's right.
I like it.
You would...
Mr. Peace and Love.
Mr. and Mrs. actually...
you know, because I have male and female sex organs.
Why am I not suprised?

meadowdrama
Ben Hertel
I should've known youre a freak...
so feminine...
I hate flowers.
Trouble with females?
No, But youre both! That's creepy.
we all have traits of both genders.
Not me! I am 100% male throughout my entire body!
I'm not so sure he believes that...
but he really wants me to.

meadowdrama
Ben Hertel
... anyway, that's why I love bees... they complete me.
will you shut up!
I feel so dirty after hearing all that!
It's nature bro.
It's disgusting! Stop talking about sex!
You're so sensitive...
you know, that's typically a female trait.
unfreakinbelieveable.....
and I thought the ice age was bad.

meadowdrama
Ben Hertel
why are you so upset ?....
so what if I'm both genders?
It's just wrong.
I have to propagate some how.
That's unseemly.
why? Because you don't do it?
I love it!
so, not only is he a lunatic...
now he's a flag waving hermaphrodite!

meadowdrama

Ben Hertel

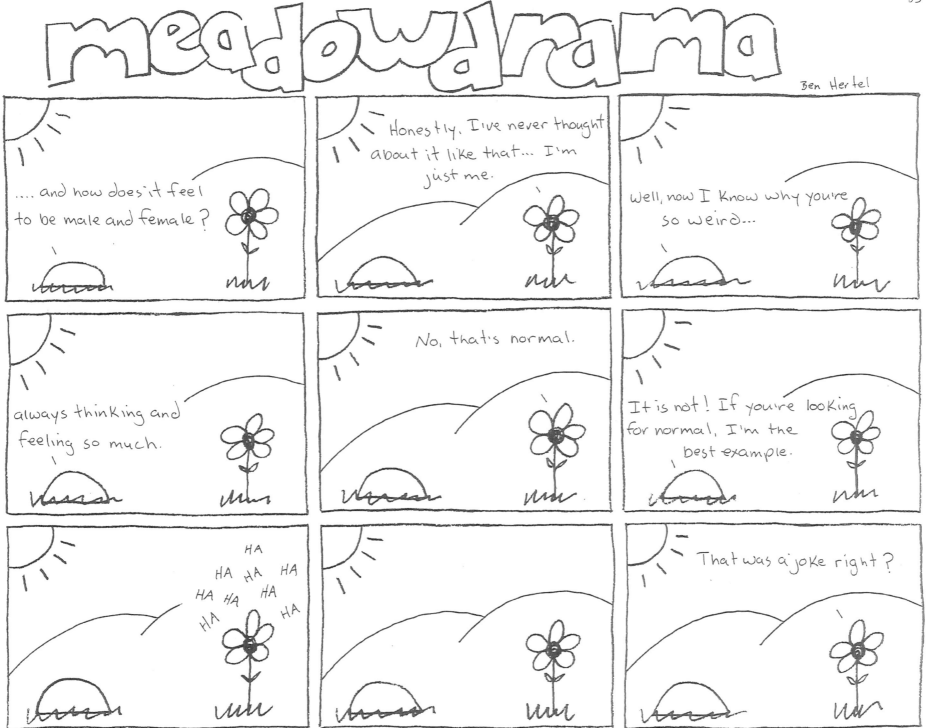

meadowdrama
Ben Hertel
You are the best example of normal?
Sure. Why not.
Angry man....
the guy that hates every body?
Hate is a valid emotion.
Yeah, but it seems to be your only emotion.
Oh! So now it's my fault that I hate all you flaming idiots?
?
Can you hear the words you are saying?!

meadowdrama
Ben Hertel
You're just jealous.
I don't think so.
Sure you are! I'm pure male, not distracted by bees, sex, or female issues.
Female issues?
Yes! Plus I can see and think clearly...
my Brain isn't full of pollen, bee cooties, and other crap...
It's totally empty!
Agreed.

meadowdrama
Ben Hertel
You are afraid of females, arn't you?...
you yell and make a big stink to cover it up....
right?
Hey. I was doing just fine until you...
had to tell me all your sex problems...
stupidgirliemanflowerthing.
You didn't answer my question.
Don't care. I can't remember it anyway.
Hmmm, must be that superiormale emptybrainthing.

meadowdrama
Ben Hertel
... life is full of mystery...
No mystery here, he's nuttier than a fruitcake.
but deep down inside we have the answers....
we just need to look.
Wrong fruitcake!
Things are obvious, no introspection required.
But, you could evolve.
I'm a rock dirt breath, what's next...
become a sidewalk?

meadowdrama
Ben Hertel
Don't you want to learn things?
I already know life is hard.
If you look beyond that there's a universe full of amazing truths.
I doubt it... anyway, change is not in my nature...
Change is for losers.
And if you don't change- it means....?
It means I win!
What...
a participation award?

meadowdrama
Ben Hertel
You can win life?
Yes!
No. I don't think that's possible.
Look at me! I'm hard as hell, attractive, solid...
and all my particles are in perfect alignment...
I'm on top! Nothing can best me!
Except paper.
? ?
It's a long story.

meadowdrama
Ben Hertel
This is my favorite part of the day...
early morning after a quiet night...
before the flower child from hell wakes up...
and starts chattering away like...
an over caffeinated squirrel on LSD.
Good morning!
Shut up. I hate you.
... he's never been much of a morning guy.

meadowdrama

Ben Hertel

Dang rock, you're so stressed you could fracture yourself.

Yeah, I've added a few worry lines over the years...

So now when it's quiet I try to empty all my thoughts...

it helps calm me down.

That would be hard for me.

you stress me out...

oh wait... I know...

and you have no clue!

you're meditating!

meadowdrama

Ben Hertel

ooooooooooooooommmmmmmmmm
oooooooooooooooommmmmmmm
ooooooooooooooommmmmmmm
what the HELL is wrong with you?!
I'm working on my meditation skills...
Om is a sacred syllable that I'm using as a mantra..
the sound vibrations resonate with your spirit and help you get centered...
and it's super fun!
I had to ask... my bad.

meadowdrama
Ben Hertel
ooooooooooooommmmmmmmm
ooooooooooooommmmmmmm
oooooooooomm—
STOP IT!
You're driving me nuts with that crap!
But it's the only way I can get into the zone.
You're always in the zone.
You think?
Sure, the 'I'm-a-lunatic-come-take-me-away' zone.

meadowdrama
Ben Hertel
Well, I guess I'm done meditating...
you have to be still for so long, and I'm more of a go, go, go kind of flower...
taking in the sun, working with the bees, so much to do...
so much to live for!
For you maybe.
Not just me, everyone!
Damn kid...
I keep trying to tell him...
but he'll never get it.

meadowdrama
Ben Hertel
Oh my! I had a really bad dream last night...
That's sad... for you.
... I was here with another flower... we were talking...
and I said 'Your color is not as bright as it should be.'
Then you died?
No... but I could have died from embarrassment!
That's your really bad dream?
Yes! I'm still pretty upset.
You are taking the word loser to a whole new level.

meadowdrama
Ben Hertel
I think you may be King of the losers.
King is good, right?
Not in this case dumbass.
Hey! That's not a very nice thing to say.
It's true. You're a disgrace to your species!
You're the most pathetic excuse for vegetation I've ever met!
Sometimes...
I think...
I could learn how to get angry.

meadowdrama
Ben Hertel
Why are we here?
Crap, not again...
I told you. To suffer and be miserable.
Well, I know that's not right...
There's too much beauty and goodness in the world.
You just need to dig around underneath all that.
misery is underneath goodness?
Yes....
I can always find it there.

meadowdrama
Ben Hertel
You're wrong about misery always being under goodness.
Dream on loser...
the more you believe that, the harder you'll fall...
when you realize I'm right.
Really?
what if you're wrong?
HA!
Crap... I'd better not be.

meadowdrama
Ben Hertel
Dude, there is love and happiness all around us...
in the sky, the water, the dirt, in the meadow...
you just need to look with an open heart.
Yeah... no thanks...
I've been a nasty old rock for a long time...
that's who I am...
and who I'll be when I turn to dust.
wow... that sounds like a life well spent...
NOT.

meadowdrama
Ben Hertel
I still hate you.
I know, it's okay.
Really?
Yeah, I've decided we're all doing the best we can...
with whatever we have to work with in this life.
So... now you're the Flower Philosopher?
Except, that kind of made sense...
and...
maybe he's not a total flaming idiot after all.

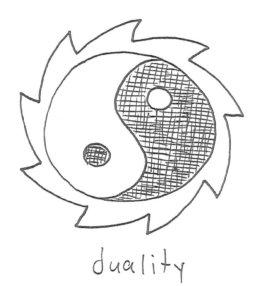

duality

CPSIA information can be obtained
www.ICGtesting.com
in the USA
07080521
00001B/1